HER VOICE

HER VOICE

poems by

Elizabeth Schultz

WOODLEY PRESS

ISBN: 0-939391-45-7

WOODLEY PRESS
Washburn University, 1700 SW College Ave., Topeka,
Kansas 66621

To
My Brother,
Howard Shaw Schultz

Contents

Beyond Seasons: The Hospital

Winter: Assisted Living

SUMMER: THE COTTAGE

MOTHER, MINE

She walks before me,
one foot placed attentively
in front of the other.

She sails before me,
her course set
by the prevailing wind.

She stands before me,
gnarled now, her skin
veined like leaves.

She sits before me,
her pinions folded
into sloping shoulders,

and I cannot hold her
though I am flesh
of her quaking flesh.

RARE BIRD

Wild still
and raptor proud,
she trusted me
to trim her feathers
into a crown
and to pluck
the sprouting bristles
around her chin,
while she grasped me
with the blue talons
of her eyes.

A HISTORY OF SWIMMING

In her father's
favorite photo,
hung above his desk,
she is swimming.
Eight-years-old,
afloat at the center
of her picture,
she makes waves
and bubbles in
abundance. She has
an otter's smirk.

A teenager,
she leaves her suit
on the shore
and swims out,
unencumbered.
Slipping through
the darkness
of water and night,
she follows the moon's
fluid flagstones.
Mercurial, she could
swim forever.

In her sixties,
neighbors watch.
She is liquid
gliding within liquid.
Hand over hand,
she strokes the lake,
its shining skin
her own. They say
she's transformed,
claimed by the lake.

She dives, testing
her depths, and rises,
arching; sunlight
glances off the sheen
of her scales.

At 95, she sinks.
With bones like
lumber, she has
become architecture
not made for water.
Estranged from fluidity,
she terrifies herself
and gasps for air.

At 96, she rises, elevated
on a Styrofoam noodle.
Once more cresting,
she reveals her secret:
swimming, after all,
is a matter of buoyancy.

LAST SUMMER

Some summer mornings
when the lake is silvered
like an old mirror,
mother stands before it,
transfixed on the dock end.
Boats float in the air
above their reflections.
A dragonfly hovers
between sky and water.
Beneath the dock, fish
float through her shadow,
and trees and cottages
on the opposite shore
appear within her grasp.

READING THE FINE LINES

In late August
certain hazy days
wipe out the lake's blue.
They rub it smooth
as pewter, leaving
a tracery of shining lines.

I try following one line.
As a breeze tarnishes
the surface, it darts east,
crisscrosses other tracks,
broadens into a southern
thoroughfare, dissolves.

This cracked glaze gives
no chart of the wind,
no scan of the water—
it is indecipherable as
the blue veins webbing
my mother's temples.

KNOTS

She insists on her work—
sweeping, feeding birds,
checking foundations,
watering saplings.

She insists on her play—
sailing, canoeing, tennis.
She knows the strokes
and some tricky moves.

But for the life of her,
she can't recall how the knot
accompanies the tale: how
the rabbit goes around the tree
and down in the hole
and comes out again.

THE GREAT GRANDMOTHER

"I sit, a reptile
in their swirl.
They bang through
the summer cottage,
tossing questions
across my stiff hide.
Like oil's slick
on the lake's surface,
they spread color.
When they must go,
I want to say,
'Stay awhile.'
They are so supple.
With my claws
and slitted eyes,
the rough scales
on my skull,
how can they guess,
I am their kin?"

RIPE FRUIT

On the shore, young
bodies ripple past.
Glossy and glowing,
succulent as apricots,
their gleam rubs off
as she sits among them.

She insists on
being in the thick
of summer's ripening.
She laps it up.
At lunch, she seizes
upon peaches, plums,
swollen into globes.
The juices dribble
haphazardly down
her dry cleavage.

Afterwards, she returns
to her stale, dark room.
The cat curls against
her body's empty socket,
while she dreams of
devouring melons whole.

ON BECOMING DEAF

First she missed
the stealth of footsteps,
the slide of pine needles,
the sounds of thrushes
shuttling through the trees.
With sound gone, the woods'
dimension diminished,
then disappeared.

Insomnia vanished when
she no longer heard
late night conversations
below her bedroom,
the branches creaking
outside her window.

Eventually the lake's winds
whisked the last voices
from her mind's chambers.
Left with a vacuous roar,
with echoes ricocheting,
and old songs throbbing,
she hummed her own storm.

ODYSSEUS' DAUGHTER

Before departing,
he taught her the ways of men and boats.
His words streamed assurance,
and she sailed alone, out of Ithaca's cove,
escaping the shore and domesticity.
Her boat trimmed, its sails tilted against
the wind impeccably as albatross wings.
She surged with dolphins across turquoise
seas,
and sitting high to windward, she rode the
horizon.

She was prepared for capsize, a loss
of rudder or sail. But she had no
grasp of the collapse at home.
Landlocked by suitors, she sat
for twenty years bound to the loom.
Through the warp of oceanic memories,
she watched for a sail on the flickering sea.

He returned at last in a blaze of sunset
and slaughtered the suitors handily.
Their corpses lay jammed on the floors.
While he idled with her mother,
she wrung out cloths and bathed
bodies for the pilgrimage to Hades.
But he, too, was gone in a flash, and
she realized only Odysseus sails forever.

COUNTDOWN

Her last summer
she watched the lake
as closely as ever.

From the pavilion,
she counted ducklings,
swimming children,
and boats at sail.

Every day, they added
up to satisfaction,
though she missed
the loons' ululations,
and the kingfishers'
blue flashes were
too quick to calculate.

Even the wind's arbitrary
wrinkling of the lake's
smooth surface proved
consequence enough,
as she circumscribed change
through her binoculars.

LOST

Near summer's end,
we set out walking deep
into a familiar woods.
My mother stumbled.

She leaned on me.
Light spattered among
the leaves overhead,
but proved no guide.

The woods became
a jigsaw puzzle
of pieces, scattered
beyond the box.

Behind and ahead,
the collective green
of fern and huckleberry
absorbed our trail.

The moss showed no
imprint. Through the grim
pines' indifference,
we flailed forward.

HER HEAD IN MY HANDS

I wash my mother's hair.
She tilts, crane-like,
toward the sink.
Her head, in my hands,
has a fragile landscape.
Blue rivers branch
over pink seas, around
small island callosities.
I massage drifting
nebulae of sensations,
unknown galaxies
of memories.
I soap her few strands
and suds them into
soggy, silken clouds.
I rinse, careful
to sluice the water
around her ears.
I finger her skull's
continents and knead
her head like terra firma.

THE VITALITY OF HER HAIR

After her death,
I found a comb,
her hair coiling up
through its teeth
with white electricity.

It was never long.
She kept it short,
out of the way,
easy to toss,
wash in a jiff,
dry in a shake,
let the wind curl.

Losing it, she
discovered vanity
and the pampering
of hairdressers.
She kept it white,
always in fashion.
Under hats she hid
permanent waves
and resistant ringlets.

At the end, she
let me trim it
out on the porch.
Strands drifted,
tangled with grass,
mingled with pine
needles, became
threads for nests,
spun into air.
Snipping done,
dandelion tufts,
gone-to-seed,
sprang from her head.

CASTING OFF

I
One day I sailed out
of my mother's hands.
I'd learned my ropes
in shallow water.
I'd practiced capsizing
and knew the dangers
of a sail held too taut,
of imbalance either
to lee or windward.

On the mother ship
she'd taught me well,
and when I cast off,
she kept watch long,
as my bark sailed
out over the stripe
of shallow blue
to be inked out soon
in deeper waters.

II
On Japan's coasts,
year after year,
in early August,
boats of curled
shavings sail down
the twisted rivers.
At each small helm,
a glowing candle
is poised to usher
souls out to sea,
their freight the names
of the beloved dead.

In Tanabe, long ago,
I watched these soul
boats set out from
that curved shore.
Like fireflies,
they flickered,
hovering above
the waves, quickening
at the horizon
into constellations.

In Tanabe, last April,
among driftwood
and the shore's grey
stones, I found
the bones of small
white stars cast up.

III
In memory,
my mother sits
high in the stern.
Grasping both
sheet and tiller,
she trims her sail.
Osprey-eyed,
she sets her course.
From dry dock,
I blow blessings
to her, but not yet,
     mother mine,
can I cast you
off among the stars.

FALL:
INDEPENDENT LIVING

FEELING IN THE DARK

Certain dark places
are familiar to me.
I can maneuver
my way to the fridge
at any time of night.
My feet have memorized
the steps. Steadily
my shadow fingers
the living room's
phantom furniture.
Plunging up against
these ghostly forms,
I have experienced
a hard knock or two.

On moonless nights,
I stroll the neighborhood,
guided by flickering
ultra blue rectangles
and erratic fireflies.
Seeing uncertainly,
I am conscious of curbs
and man-shaped shrubs.

But when my upright
mother crumpled
mid-day in the street,
I lost my familiar footing.
Against the asphalt,
her jack-knifed body
sprawled abstractly.
Unable to re-arrange,
much less interpret
this new design, I was
left, feeling in the dark.

FEAR OF FALLING

You used to tumble
and bounce on concrete.
You skinned both knees,
and with aplomb, pooh-
poohed your bruises.
You fell out of bed,
off boats, and in love.
You fell with grace, until,
cracking and fracturing,
you couldn't put yourself
back together again.

You hesitate now to walk
across grass, afraid of
anthills and mole-tunnels.
You stand quizzically
at the top of escalators
as their stairs unpleat.
You envision friends
disassembled in bath tubs.
You remember how
Daedalus was warned
of the terrible rushing
of air, the ground rising
and bones splintering.

GRACIOUS LIVING

Beyond the bay window,
the snow drifted affably
on the apple tree's decaying stump.
It powdered the two pines,
now roof-high, pampered seedlings
when the house was new.

Inside, mother sorted
silver, crystal, porcelain,
ninety-years' accumulation,
intricate and gleaming.
Cordially, she greeted each item,
then, one by one, let them
go as easily as a first
frost melts on a pane.

SATISFACTION

After the family mansion
of many rooms, she finds
one to be enough: walls
with a door and windows
to open and close at will.

From shelves of books,
she chooses the dictionary:
it contains all necessary
words and meanings.

Sapphires and silver urns
she bequeaths to others,
while the platinum ring
circling her third finger
becomes the merest wire.

In the center of her room,
she seats herself and stakes
her claim to light and dark.
Her hands lie in her lap,
clasped as bivalves,
cupping satisfaction.

CLAIMING BAGGAGE

Dazed in this new space
of vacant vistas and closed doors,
she believed she'd strayed into
a hotel's anonymity, where plastic
flowers were beauty's measure.

She wandered echoing corridors,
lost luggage scooting around
on a conveyor belt, her identity a tag.
Faces called her. Glad hands slapped
announcements into her pockets
and pushed her into an elevator.

Beeps and buzzers, and they gushed
out together into the well-upholstered
lobby, where, remembering her social
graces, she picked herself up by
her own handle, and walked clear
into falling light.

DOING THE DISHES

Since she started
service to housewifery,
mother performed
the dish sacrament
three times daily.
Faded, green-checked
apron, her vestment,
high priestess of
the house, she handled
cups and saucers
as sacred vessels.

She engaged us all
in stacking, rinsing,
soaking, washing
dishes with decorum.
Passing each one on
to us, her acolytes,
she trained us to restore
them to appointed shelves.
She codified and purified
our family practices.

Alone now, she does
not resort to apostasy.
She explores new rituals,
twirling dishes through
the foaming suds and
spinning by herself
in the kitchenette.

Her Tools

She said, "I still might
make another little cake,"
but was persuaded
to let the Mix-Master go.

Other tools accompanied her.
Best friends
and more reliable than kids,
they remain handy.

Pliers, hammer, screwdriver,
polished by use, familiar
to the touch, line up
at the sink, primed for action.

Spatulas, knives, ladles,
nicked in everyday fray,
bed down in drawers,
ready to rise when called.

The brass bowl holds,
as always, an assortment—
rubber bands, pins, tape—
more certain than words
for making connections.

THE SECRETARY

Tier on tier, shelves
and drawers rose up
in the family secretary.
Attentive at the altar,
mother pigeon-holed
a rambunctious past,
laid out the anxious present
in immaculate rows.
Fingering the future,
she organized eternity
in detailed ledgers,
but always kept its secrets
and reliquaries obscure.

She did not reckon
on the shifting winds
in the canyons
of her mind, nor
the avalanches of spies
and assassins which
would rumble through
its orderly gardens.
The high dome cracked,
and stories crashed.
With ravaged logic,
she stashed her will
between sofa cushions.

THE DUBIOUS ADVANTAGES OF HEARING AIDS

She desired muffled memories:
the hush of snow beating light
wings against her windows,
the sigh of a lake lapping a shore.
She had cancelled cacophony.

When suddenly, the room roared
with natural disasters: the refrigerator
gurgling up a tsunami, the furnace
clunking into an avalanche, newspapers
rustling earthquakes. And everyone
shouting as if her life were in danger.

TIME AND TEMPERATURE

She dismisses calendars
and engagement books.
Anniversaries and birthdays
have been scrapped.
Doomsday may be tomorrow.
The daily news, unread,
drifts into dust balls.

It is enough to know
the time is five-fifteen.
She turns her cuff back
over the wrist watch,
and glances toward
the porch thermometer
where the temperature is
steady, just above freezing.

Released from history
and into the heat
of her own instant,
she watches the winter
sky go up in flames,
and the crows scissor
through unscathed.
She checks again:
the time is five-sixteen;
the temperature holds
for now.

NOBLE SAVAGES

Their breathing
seethes inside the lair.
Through the day,
the old woman and
her cat hibernate
in a woolen coil:
laps for each other.

Drool innocently
pearls on their
lips, and puddles
on sweater and fur.
They shift together,
stretching into
dreams of satiation,
performing yoga
in their sleep.

They wake to nuzzle
and to flex their
paunches. Eating is
smacking, crunching,
and sipping with
metered deliberation.

Startled, they bristle
with fang and claw—
fast to snap and
fast to curl back
into creature comfort.

SHE CHOOSES LIGHT

She chooses light.
As noiseless as
a narcissus opening
in a bowl of pebbles,
it enters the room.

She watches light stroke
the family photos,
the ancient afghan,
her favorite books.
It leaves no fingerprints.

Her eyelids flickering,
momentarily she flirts
with shades, but accepts
light's down comforter,
easing up over the couch.

She dozes among its glowing
folds and misses the shadows
of clouds billowing through
the room and the dark patches
of crows passing.

WINTER GRASSES

In spring and summer,
they learn suppleness,
scrolling across fields,
sashaying and swaying,
composing with the wind.

In autumn, they flare
into various crimsons.
They also rust, stiffen,
stoop with the weight
of seeds.

Now in winter,
they relax, letting
rhizomes and memory
stretch out underground.

Above the snow,
they clack and chatter,
despite their tatters.

Some slouch back easily
into yellow arcs,
and a pale sun teases
their empty tassels.
They've never been
so light-headed

Beyond Seasons:
The Hospital

Mother Tongue

"It is what, that thing,
I put it there, so whenever
I'd need it, sometimes I
just wanted to tell you in case.
I stretch my arms and
shape it wide, but cannot
grasp the thing itself."

CATCHING THE DRIFT

Unanchored, words
drift into depths
beyond markings.
Sentences open up
to baffling breezes.
Names carry cargo,
too heavy to lift.

Such blabbering,
such bubbling.
You pucker up,
blow words into air.

They float free in
cartoon balloons.
They bounce toward me.
I bend forward,
try snatching them,
swallowing them,
repeating after you
before they escape
beyond the horizon.

BORDER-CROSSING

We come bereft to this new land.
Mother's purse, sole remnant, perches
in her lap. We wheel her, paralyzed,
across the threshold. We have left
the vestiges of yesterday behind:
> shifting aromas,
> blushing fruit,
> breezes.

We come desperate to this new land.
We pass from cubicle to cubicle.
The guides for hire speak another
language. Without compass
and notes from previous immigrants,
we wander. We debate diverse
destinations. We trespass into
desert and confusion. We are stymied.
With our furious queries, we are
quarantined in cells until authority
stamps our passports of uncertainty.

We prepare for an arduous crossing.
We seek the comfort of familiar signs:
> omniscient moon by night,
> geese unraveling by day,
> greetings in the morning,
> blessings in the evening.
Inured against hope, we hold hands.
Mother leads us, faltering forward,
her eyes rounding in innocence,
as we trip into this age-old country.

SEEKING PARADISE

Amidst the E.R.'s roar,
sequestered, behind curtains,
mother, patient as sand,
lies attached to seething tubes.

In the corridor, the medics
bring in a woman, one
to each corner of her bier.
An immense loaf of flesh,
she rises up in outrage
from her winding sheets,
revealing shoulders and arms,
tattooed purple and red
with daggers and dragons.
She cusses and spits,
and her great moon face
splits in ferocious grimace,
as they wheel her away.

Lagoon blue veins creep
quietly around mother's skull,
snake down her arms, come
full bloom on her hands
as hematoid orchids.
She sucks ice placidly
and watches for angel fish
to drift across the ceiling.
She asks if this is paradise.

BIRTH ANNOUNCEMENT

Delivery into eternity
is profound labor.
In the long gestation
of dying, she emerges
infantile once more,
dependent and cranky.
Her hair, source of
vanity and sexual
distinction, goes—
scalp and pubes now
as bald as any babe's.
Her skin, with its foxed
cartography, droops
in thin tissue folds.
At the crib edge, she
prattles an endless tune,
and cerulean blue eyes
drift toward infinity.
Diapered and spoon-fed,
her docile body curls
into the fetal comma.
Only callused heels
and long curved nails
give her away to time.

PROFILING

They did not see
her domed forehead,
her beaked nose,
and soft chin
in immutable profile.

They saw the skull
packaged by skin
thin as cellophane.

They did not know
her hands' competence,
capable of intricate
stitching and splicing.

They did not imagine
the grace implicit
in her arched feet.

Perceiving only
sagging outlines,
they branded her
shopworn, discounted,
and predicted decline.

They left her, then,
to hang on the rack.

SHANGHAIED

Shackled by I.V. tubes
and oxygen lines twisted
like hawsers across
her chest, she's caught
naked on a pirate raft.

She watches them
whispering, bringing
hardtack and grog, but
keeps her mouth locked,
throws away the key,
resists keel-hauling.

Before she knows it,
a parade's going by,
calliopes beeping,
elephants tramping,
antelopes on trapezes.

Spangles and sequins
sparkle; flags fly on
every T-shirt. Sighting
the bearded lady, she
asks aloud what it's
like to grow whiskers.

If only she had her clothes,
she would join them.
But the pirates have
stolen her robe, and
the parade fades,
leaving her tangled
in dangling threads.

QUEEN MOTHER

Kowtowing, the generations come.
They encircle the bed where she presides.

Offerings of candies, hard as jewels,
and tinsel hearts are spread out before her.

The ancient scent of piss and saliva rises
stealthily from golden urns secreted
beneath her.

Upon her wrinkled sheets, acolytes strew
sweets
from fast-food machines, and executing
affection,

they dance and twist their karaoke
routines.
Amidst elaborate trappings of coiled tubes,

enthroned in solemnity,
she performs her strenuous smile.

LOVE, O CARELESS, CARELESS LOVE

Our contagious kisses,
infectious smooches,
strangling embraces,
suffocating sentiments,
we confess to at last,
seeing love itself reduced
to bedsores and spittle.

OBATE*

Heavier on my back
than any firewood,
my mother digs her
heels into my sides,
goads me forward.

On the grooved trail
the snow is deep,
the mountain steep.

All my childhood years
she'd back-packed me
about the village,
into the fields,
feeding me sweets
over her shoulder
along our way.

She clings, choking
my throat with talons.

I stumble, shifting
my ferocious burden,
shivering to think
she has a beast's
survival strength.

The snow is deeper,
the mountain steeper.

She's become a boulder.

She doesn't moan.

I hear myself bleat
in the home vernacular,
offering her a rice cake.

Her silence prods me on.

On the white mountain,
the cave's mouth gapes,
our inevitable end.

This bundle of mother
I set down on the lip,
among ancestral bones.

She assembles herself,
a Buddha already,
and together we wait
for ravens and vultures
to come pick us clean.

*The ritual in feudal Japan whereby an adult child
brought a dying parent into the mountains to die

CAPTURING THE ORYX

Skittish and shy,
she was a creature
I'd not seen before.
Her face bolted,
she stared, aghast
out of the shadows.

Perhaps she recalled
the fertile savannah
and the elegant touch
of egrets on her haunches.
In our sterile air,
she snorted lavishly.

Desperate to please,
I tried caressing
her twitching hide.
She shook off
my pawing.
I tried kissing
her downy cheek.
Her long blue tongue
lashed at my lips.

I went down, kneeled
at her feet, lifted
a hoof into my hands.
Split into shards,
its arch held a history
of prancing.

For days, I subdued
her body's hard agony
with unguent perfumes
and oils, until haltered
by my soothing ways,
I led her into the cage.

IN HER ABSENCE

In the early morning light
my shadow trespasses across her space
lingers on a cherished engraving,
elongates over the table, set for one.
It crosses the kitchen cupboards,
polishes a pot upon the stove.
It irons her dangling apron,
and fondles her patched potholders.
It searches in vain, missing her
everywhere.

WINTER:
ASSISTED LIVING

CAGED RAPTOR

She resists, enraged
by perpetual light.
She sees no death
in the glittering day.

In perpetual light,
her needs exposed
to the glittering day,
she swoops down.

Her needs exposed,
she rattles her wings
and swoops down
among the sparrows.

She rattles her wings,
ignoring the clatter
among the sparrows,
snared by brightness.

Ignoring the clatter,
she circles the aviary,
snared by brightness
within these bars.

She circles the aviary,
summoning darkness,
and within these bars,
is hooded on her perch.

Summoning darkness,
she rests from glare,
hooded on her perch,
but dying persists.

Resting from glare,
she sees no death,
but dying persists.
She resists, enraged.

LIVING ROOM

With other residents,
she sits before a screen,
leaping with dogs
in carnival hats.

As if on strings,
her feet dangle
from the wheelchair.
She tilts her head.

Precisely, she selects
a bingo ball to taste.
She explains if you ask:
"This is the truth:

I am 110. I died at 97."
Then, this must be
paradise, you suggest.
"No," she corrects,

"This is the living room."

DYING DREAMS

Her body dissolved.
Chilled by the gap
below her neck,
she woke to death.
She spoke its name
and lived to tell us.

She left us often
to converse with
luminous wraiths.
Like summer moths
about a porch light,
they fluttered into
her dusky sphere.
"Your Dad was here,"
she said, " but he's
taking a dip now."
Through the day,
she heard them
singing, gathered in
memory's outposts.

Former visions of
derring-do and narrow
escape had vanished.
Instead, she checked
on her own funeral:
a celebratory affair.
Music, flowers, guests
fulfilled her dreams.
If only she could die.

GOLDILOCKS

As in any hotel,
the corridors are
padded passageways,
lined with blank doors.
Names posted above
numbers are runes
in unknown language.
In her wheelchair,
she cruises the corridors,
discovering limits.

Recognizing no one,
she wonders what
her business is.
She glides through
a lounge, waving
to sedate strangers,
propelling herself
down another hall,
forward into vacuity.

Exhausted by such
soft anonymity,
she enters a room,
duplicate of the one
she left this morning.
She places her glasses
on the nightstand,
and cautiously tests
her neighbor's bed.

IN A FRENCH HOTEL

She scoots down
the hall, the walker
in front of her
a hefty cow catcher.
Before she crashes,
she hollers her name,
"Lucy, not Lucille."
With desperate gaiety,
she is running away.

She flashes her nails,
orangutan orange,
painted by a stranger
who enjoys color.
"Coral," she advertises,
camouflaging confusion
in carnival, and adjusting
a pointed birthday hat.

She beams and smears
fudge frosting thick as
rouge on her cheeks.
"Parlez-vous français,"
she sings out recklessly.
It all comes back now.
She's just arrived
in a French hotel
and should be home
again any day.

A Simple Rock

With barking in her ears,
yapping at her heels,
she chooses a stone
for concentration.
It is quiet and grey
like a cat asleep
at the foot of her bed.
It can be petted, rubbed,
obsessively smoothed.
It reveals only itself,
soothing and still.

SIGNATURE

In wavering dashes,
she first named
herself on paper.

Over time, she refined
her line and signed into
life with a dignified flare.

Rejoicing to add a curl
and downward zooms
with strong parallels,
she annexed a husband.

The signature showed
her hand, competent,
confident, eccentric,
and claiming multiple texts.

Today she sits, letting
zeroes roll, line after line,
scrolling like waves over
her blank page as if she knew
we're all writ on water.

THE MOUTH

Chewing,
spitting,
sucking,
sighing,
shouting,
swallowing,
smirking,
smacking,
smiling,
smooching,
slurping,
sipping,
gnawing,
hacking,
hollering,
hemming,
hawing,
pursing,
puckering,
twisting,
kissing,
expectorating,
the mouth
does it all:
entrance, egress.
It takes it in,
gives it out:
breath, spit,
food, water,
words, kisses.
Rosebud,
trapdoor,
little line,
black hole,
the mouth
opens and
closes her.

GONE WILD

Her body has gone wild.
Its wrinkled turf is
rugged, overgrown
with excrescences.
A foreign landscape,
its slopes and divides
sprout alien warts.
Blotches bloom in
faded rose and violet.

Seeking the familiar
terrain of self, she tries
to tame unruliness
with salves and creams.
Monthly, a podiatrist
trims her barnacles,
and on Thursdays,
a beautician puffs up
her tufts of hair.

Nothing prevents
pubic hairs from
trekking to her chin.
They bristle with
cactus masculinity.
She fingers familiar
creases and crevices,
perplexed by the terrain
she's crossing now.

HER BREASTS

Dressed by class and inhibition,
for decades she harnessed
and concealed her breasts.

Hammocked against her chest,
she kept their stories close:
their ripening bloom,
their tingling in cold springs,
their swelling with thick milk,
and in summer's heat, how
she allowed them to sashay unbound.

Strangers' chilly hands cup them
now; indifferent eyes bruise them.
Feeling them droop and tremble,
dismissed as outmoded appendages,
before sleep, then, she gathers them in,
bouquets of full-blown peonies.

BETRAYAL

Uncertain where she is,
she locates me securely
in her childhood, just arriving
from her hometown, acquainted
with her playmates. She tells
them I've come, bearing sweets.

She can't see
I am a wooden horse,
duplicitous and sneaky,
reasoning with her memories,
cajoling her with chocolate.
She pops grapes into her mouth,
one after another. Her eyes gleam
like a young squirrel's.

She can't guess
I will abandon her repeatedly
behind the cut-glass door.
She sits in her wheel-chair,
magnified and multiplied.
I leave her stranded
in innocence, blowing me
a thousand silent kisses.

SHE DOESN'T LIVE HERE ANYMORE

When I arrive, she takes me in.
Effortlessly, she walks through
doors and walls into familiar rooms.

She greets her mother and father,
in the bright dining room, and going up
stairs, calls out for her sister.

Answering, I discuss the weather
which we both observe outside
her window: overcast and charged.

She leaves by the backdoor, and
in a barn hollowed out by fear,
once more she's forced onto the straw.

Held down, she watches the swallows
above her, slipping through long streaks
of light. Soundlessly, she screams.

She runs then, around the corner,
over and over again, passing playmates,
under the old trees, until she finds me.

No one must know. I pass a glass of water,
and we open the book of family photographs.
We look at the old house and barn.

When I leave, she waves from the threshold.
I close her door and promise to return,
although she doesn't live here anymore.

GONE HOME

Locked in,
she confronts a door.
Beyond is a field
of ravaged stalks
and a traffic light
relentlessly blinking.
Geese glide in, one
layer after another.
She watches them
squat and gabble.
In some other life,
she might choose
goose contentment.
But her mother's
voice carols through
the corridors, calling
her to sunrise.
She tests the door's
elaborate handle.
Without opening it,
she's already reached
her destination.

JANUARY DEATH

Stepping into death,
her feet froze first.
Tableclothed in snow,
the lake invited her.

She upset the crystals
crocheting the shore,
disturbed a tide-pool,
a gelid goblet suspended
between ice and sand.
She shivered, then
slipped coolly beneath
the whiteness.

Flushed with chill
she spread out her
lavender hands and
opened her eyes to
fish bigger than life.

HER VOICE

I can consider what song
my mother would sing
if we were driving,
and what she'd say
about the snow falling.

But I no longer hear
her sing, hear her speak.
Like her unique ear
whorls and thumbprint,
her voice has vanished.

Lacking guttural or nasal
distinction or a bird's
specific chirp or caw,
it sounds no echoes now,
no ringing in the air.

I eavesdrop on
the night sky's silence,
and yearning for
resonance, press my ear
against mute memory.

The author gratefully acknowledges the following journals for their previous publication of her poems: *Iota* for "*Obate*," *Seeding the Snow* for "Winter Grasses," *Rockhurst Review* for "She Doesn't Live Here Anymore" and "Odysseus' Daughter." She also wishes to thank Vic Contoski, Joe Harrington, Dick Schoeck, Brian Daldorph, Denise Low, Mary Wharff, and Harriet Lerner, for their enlightening comments on the manuscript. Finally, this book would not have been possible without the support and assistance of Pam LeRow and Gary Lechliter.

Elizabeth Schultz retired in 2001 from the University of Kansas, where she was the Chancellor's Club Teaching Professor in the English Department. The author of *Unpainted to the Last: Moby-Dick and Twentieth-Century American Art* (1995) and *Shoreline: Seasons at the Lake* (2001), she has published extensively in the fields of nineteenth-century American fiction, American women's writing, African American fiction and autobiography, and Japanese culture. A founder of the Melville Society Cultural Project, she has curated several exhibitions related to Melville and the arts, and has co-edited a collection of essays on Melville and women (2006). She has also written *Conversations: Art into Poetry at the Spencer Museum of Art* (2006).

www.ingramcontent.com/pod-product-compliance
Lightning Source LLC
Chambersburg PA
CBHW032210040426

42449CB00005B/524